A

Christian is…

ROBENS CHERY

A Christian Is

Copyright © 2023 by Robens Chery

Publisher: Principle House Publishing
             P.O. Box 190453
             Lauderhill, Florida 33319

Cover design, interior design, and formatting by Evoke180 Publishing
A Christian Is/Robens Chery
ISBN 978-1-7379938-8-9

Name:

_____

Date

_____

Organization

_____

TABLE OF CONTENTS

INTRODUCTION

It's an honor to be called a Christian. Christians are followers of Jesus Christ who dedicate their lives to spread the gospel to every corner of the globe. Calling ourselves Christians is more than just a name, it's a lifestyle.

So what is a Christian? Billions of people all over the world claim to be a Christian, but their beliefs, doctrines, and practices vary.

What does being a Christian mean? Let's take a quick look at what a Christian is.

Definition of Christian

1a: one who professes belief in the teachings of Jesus Christ.

1b: disciple

What is the origin of the word Christian?

It is of Latin origin, and the meaning of Christian is "follower of Christ" from Latin Christianus. Christ is from Greek Khristos, a translation of the Hebrew term, "Messiah," meaning "anointed." Christian and Christiana were used for women in medieval times, but by the 18th century, Christina was the more common form.

The word Christian is used three times in the New Testament (*Acts 11:26, 1 Peter 4:16, Revelation 2:10*).

"And when he had found him, he brought him to Antioch. And it came to pass, that a whole year they assembled themselves with the church, and taught much people. The disciples were called Christians first in Antioch." ***Acts 11:26***

There's a responsibility that comes with calling ourselves Christians. God is calling us to follow His son Jesus Christ because in Him, we may be reconciled to the father. This responsibility requires boldness with

our daily walk. Although it can get very difficult at times, we are called to expand the kingdom of God here on earth by living righteously on a consistent basis. I pray that this book will be a daily remainder of our faith as Christians in a world full of confusion and uncertainties. May God grant you the ability to stand and proclaim the gospel of Jesus Christ as we await His second coming.

A Christian is.....

Quote #1

TO BELIEVE THAT JESUS IS THE SON OF GOD.

"FOR GOD SO LOVED THE WORLD THAT HE GAVE HIS ONE AND ONLY SON, THAT WHOEVER BELIEVES IN HIM SHALL NOT PERISH BUT HAVE ETERNAL LIFE."

JOHN 3:16 NIV

Quote #2

TO ACCEPT AND DECLARE JESUS CHRIST AS YOUR LORD AND SAVIOR.

"IF YOU DECLARE WITH YOUR MOUTH, "JESUS IS LORD," AND BELIEVE IN YOUR HEART THAT GOD RAISED HIM FROM THE DEAD, YOU WILL BE SAVED."

ROMANS 10:9 NIV

Quote #3

TO BELIEVE THAT JESUS DIED ON THE CROSS FOR OUR SINS.

www.robenschery.com

"BUT GOD DEMONSTRATES HIS OWN LOVE FOR US IN THIS: WHILE WE WERE STILL SINNERS, CHRIST DIED FOR US."

ROMANS 5:8 NIV

Quote #4

TO BE A FOLLOWER OF JESUS CHRIST.

"THEN JESUS SAID TO HIS DISCIPLES, "WHOEVER WANTS TO BE MY DISCIPLE MUST DENY THEMSELVES AND TAKE UP THEIR CROSS AND FOLLOW ME."

MATTHEW 16:24 NIV

Quote #5

TO BELIEVE THAT JESUS CHRIST IS THE MESSIAH.

"BUT THESE ARE WRITTEN THAT YOU MAY BELIEVE THAT JESUS IS THE MESSIAH, THE SON OF GOD, AND THAT BY BELIEVING YOU MAY HAVE LIFE IN HIS NAME."

JOHN 20:31 NIV

Quote #6

TO REPENT FROM YOUR SINS DAILY.

www.robenschery.com

**"IF WE CONFESS OUR SINS, HE IS FAITH-
FUL AND JUST AND WILL FORGIVE
US OUR SINS AND PURIFY US FROM
ALL UNRIGHTEOUSNESS."**

1 JOHN 1:9 NIV

Quote #7

TO TRUST IN GOD.

**"TRUST IN THE LORD WITH ALL
YOUR HEART AND LEAN NOT ON
YOUR OWN UNDERSTANDING."**

PROVERBS 3:5 NIV

Quote #8

TO BE BORN AGAIN.

JESUS REPLIED, "VERY TRULY I TELL YOU, NO ONE CAN SEE THE KINGDOM OF GOD UNLESS THEY ARE BORN AGAIN."

JOHN 3:3 NIV

Quote #9

TO LOVE YOUR ENEMIES.

"BUT I TELL YOU, LOVE YOUR ENEMIES AND PRAY FOR THOSE WHO PERSECUTE YOU."

MATTHEW 5:44 NIV

Quote #10

TO LOVE ONE ANOTHER.

"A NEW COMMAND I GIVE YOU: LOVE ONE ANOTHER AS I HAVE LOVED YOU, SO YOU MUST LOVE ONE ANOTHER. BY THIS EVERYONE WILL KNOW THAT YOU ARE MY DISCIPLES, IF YOU LOVE ONE ANOTHER."

JOHN 13:34-35 NIV

Quote #11

TO FORGIVE ONE ANOTHER.

www.robenschery.com

Quote #12

TO CARE FOR ONE ANOTHER.

"DEAR FRIENDS, LET US LOVE ONE ANOTHER, FOR LOVE COMES FROM GOD. EVERYONE WHO LOVES HAS BEEN BORN OF GOD AND KNOWS GOD."

1 JOHN 4:7 NIV

Quote #13

NOT TO FOLLOW THE WORLD.

"DO NOT LOVE THE WORLD OR ANYTHING IN THE WORLD. IF ANYONE LOVES THE WORLD, LOVE FOR THE FATHER IS NOT IN THEM."

1 JOHN 2:15 NIV

Quote #14

TO BE BAPTIZED.

**PETER REPLIED, "REPENT AND BE BAP-
TIZED, EVERY ONE OF YOU, IN THE NAME
OF JESUS CHRIST FOR THE FORGIVENESS
OF YOUR SINS. AND YOU WILL RECEIVE
THE GIFT OF THE HOLY SPIRIT."**

ACTS 2:38 NIV

Quote #15

TO BELIEVE THAT WE ARE ALL CHILDREN OF GOD.

"SUPPOSE ONE OF YOU WANTS TO BUILD A TOWER. WON'T YOU FIRST SIT DOWN AND ESTIMATE THE COST TO SEE IF YOU HAVE ENOUGH MONEY TO COMPLETE IT?"

LUKE 14:28 NIV

Quote #16

TO BE A GOOD STEWARD OVER OUR GIFTS.

**"EACH OF YOU SHOULD USE WHATEV-
ER GIFT YOU HAVE RECEIVED TO SERVE
OTHERS, AS FAITHFUL STEWARDS OF
GOD'S GRACE IN ITS VARIOUS FORMS."**

1 PETER 4:10 NIV

Quote #17

TO BE A CHRISTIAN EVERYDAY OF THE WEEK, NOT JUST ON SUNDAY.

www.robenschery.com

"THEN HE SAID TO THEM ALL: "WHOEVER WANTS TO BE MY DISCIPLE MUST DENY THEMSELVES AND TAKE UP THEIR CROSS DAILY AND FOLLOW ME."

LUKE 9:23 NIV

Quote #18

TO FOLLOW JESUS CHRIST NOT RELIGION.

"JESUS ANSWERED, "I AM THE WAY AND THE TRUTH AND THE LIFE. NO ONE COMES TO THE FATHER EXCEPT THROUGH ME."

JOHN 14:6 NIV

Quote #19

TO HAVE A PERSONAL RELATIONSHIP WITH CHRIST.

"HERE I AM! I STAND AT THE DOOR AND KNOCK. IF ANYONE HEARS MY VOICE AND OPENS THE DOOR, I WILL COME IN AND EAT WITH THAT PERSON, AND THEY WITH ME."

REVELATION 3:20 NIV

Quote #20

TO BE READY TO BE TALKED ABOUT.

www.robenschery.com

**"IF YOU ARE INSULTED BECAUSE
OF THE NAME OF CHRIST, YOU ARE
BLESSED, FOR THE SPIRIT OF GLORY
AND OF GOD RESTS ON YOU."**

1 PETER 4:14 NIV

Quote #21

TO BE READY TO BE PERSECUTED.

"BLESSED ARE THOSE WHO ARE PERSE-CUTED BECAUSE OF RIGHTEOUSNESS, FOR THEIRS IS THE KINGDOM OF HEAVEN."

MATTHEW 5:10 NIV

Quote #22

TO BE A DISCIPLE
OF CHRIST.

"THEREFORE GO AND MAKE DISCI-PLES OF ALL NATIONS, BAPTIZING THEM IN THE NAME OF THE FATHER AND OF THE SON AND OF THE HOLY SPIRIT."

MATTHEW 28:19 NIV

Quote #23

TO BE READY TO BE MISUNDERSTOOD.

"HANNAH WAS PRAYING IN HER HEART, AND HER LIPS WERE MOVING BUT HER VOICE WAS NOT HEARD. ELI THOUGHT SHE WAS DRUNK."

1 SAMUEL 1:13 NIV

Quote #24

NOT TO GIVE UP IN TIME OF HARDSHIP.

"I HAVE LABORED AND TOILED AND HAVE OFTEN GONE WITHOUT SLEEP; I HAVE KNOWN HUNGER AND THIRST AND HAVE OFTEN GONE WITHOUT FOOD; I HAVE BEEN COLD AND NAKED."

2 CORINTHIANS 11:26-27 NIV

Quote #25

TO RESPOND TO THE CALLING OF GOD.

"BUT YOU ARE A CHOSEN PEOPLE, A ROYAL PRIESTHOOD, A HOLY NATION, GOD'S SPECIAL POSSESSION, THAT YOU MAY DECLARE THE PRAISES OF HIM WHO CALLED YOU OUT OF DARKNESS INTO HIS WONDERFUL LIGHT."

1 PETER 2:9 NIV

Quote #26

TO FOLLOW KINGDOM PRINCIPLES.

www.robenschery.com

"YOUR KINGDOM COME, YOUR WILL BE DONE, ON EARTH AS IT IS IN HEAVEN."

MATTHEW 6:10 NIV

Quote #27

TO TAKE RESPONSIBILITY FOR YOUR ACTIONS.

www.robenschery.com

"SO THEN, EACH OF US WILL GIVE AN ACCOUNT OF OURSELVES TO GOD."

ROMANS 14:12 NIV

Quote #28

NOT ABOUT COLOR OR RACE.

"FOR GOD SO LOVED THE WORLD THAT HE GAVE HIS ONE AND ONLY SON, THAT WHOEVER BELIEVES IN HIM SHALL NOT PERISH BUT HAVE ETERNAL LIFE."

JOHN 3:16 NIV

Quote #29

NOT ABOUT TRADITION, BUT ABOUT RE-LATIONSHIP.

"JESUS REPLIED, "AND WHY DO YOU BREAK THE COMMAND OF GOD FOR THE SAKE OF YOUR TRADITION?"

MATTHEW 15:3 NIV

Quote #30

TO BE READY TO BE DEPENDENT ON CHRIST.

"THAT IS WHY, FOR CHRIST'S SAKE, I DELIGHT IN WEAKNESSES, IN INSULTS, IN HARDSHIPS, IN PERSECUTIONS, IN DIFFICULTIES. FOR WHEN I AM WEAK, THEN I AM STRONG."

2 CORINTHIANS 12:10 NIV

Quote #31

TO BE READY TO BE HATED BY THE WORLD.

"IF THE WORLD HATES YOU, KEEP IN MIND THAT IT HATED ME FIRST."

JOHN 15:18 NIV

Quote #32

TO HAVE FAITH.

**"AND WITHOUT FAITH IT IS IMPOSSI-
BLE TO PLEASE GOD, BECAUSE ANYONE
WHO COMES TO HIM MUST BELIEVE
THAT HE EXISTS AND THAT HE REWARDS
THOSE WHO EARNESTLY SEEK HIM."**

HEBREWS 11:6 NIV

Quote #33

TO ENDURE HARDSHIP.

"YOU WILL BE HATED BY EVERYONE BECAUSE OF ME, BUT THE ONE WHO ENDURES TO THE END WILL BE SAVED."

MATTHEW 10:22 NIV

Quote #34

TO DIE TO SELF EVERYDAY.

"THEN HE SAID TO THEM ALL: "WHOEVER WANTS TO BE MY DISCIPLE MUST DENY THEMSELVES AND TAKE UP THEIR CROSS DAILY AND FOLLOW ME."

LUKE 9:23 NIV

Quote #35

TO READ THE WORD DAILY.

"YOUR WORD IS A LAMP FOR MY FEET, A LIGHT ON MY PATH."

PSALMS 119:105 NIV

Quote #36

TO WORSHIP GOD AND GOD ALONE.

www.robenschery.com

"COME, LET US BOW DOWN IN WORSHIP, LET US KNEEL BEFORE THE LORD OUR MAKER."

PSALMS 95:6 NIV

Quote #37

TO HAVE NO OTHER GOD.

**"YOU SHALL HAVE NO OTHER
GODS BEFORE ME."**

EXODUS 20:3 NIV

Quote #38

TO DEVELOP A RELA-TIONSHIP WITH GOD.

"WE PROCLAIM TO YOU WHAT WE HAVE SEEN AND HEARD, SO THAT YOU ALSO MAY HAVE FELLOWSHIP WITH US. AND OUR FELLOWSHIP IS WITH THE FATHER AND WITH HIS SON, JESUS CHRIST."

1 JOHN 1:3 NIV

Quote #39

TO ESTABLISH GOD'S KINGDOM, POWER, AND AUTHORITY HERE ON EARTH.

"FOR THE KINGDOM OF GOD IS NOT A MATTER OF TALK BUT OF POWER."

1 CORINTHIANS 4:20 NIV

Quote #40

TO DEMONSTRATE THE KINGDOM OF GOD ON EARTH.

"FOR THE KINGDOM OF GOD IS NOT A MATTER OF EATING AND DRINKING, BUT OF RIGHTEOUSNESS, PEACE AND JOY IN THE HOLY SPIRIT."

ROMANS 14:17 NIV

Quote #41

TO EXPAND THE KINGDOM OF GOD WITH YOUR RESOURCES.

"ALL THE BELIEVERS WERE TOGETH-ER AND HAD EVERYTHING IN COMMON. THEY SOLD PROPERTY AND POSSESSIONS TO GIVE TO ANYONE WHO HAD NEED."

ACTS 2:44-45 NIV

Quote #42

TO BELIEVE THAT GOD IS THE CREATOR OF ALL THINGS.

"IN THE BEGINNING GOD CREATED THE HEAVENS AND THE EARTH."

GENESIS 1:1 NIV

Quote #43

TO BELIEVE THAT JESUS CAME FROM GOD.

"THE WORD BECAME FLESH AND MADE HIS DWELLING AMONG US. WE HAVE SEEN HIS GLORY, THE GLORY OF THE ONE AND ONLY SON, WHO CAME FROM THE FATHER, FULL OF GRACE AND TRUTH."

JOHN 1:14 NIV

Quote #44

TO BE A GOOD STEWARD OVER OUR FINANCES.

**JESUS SAID, "LET THE LITTLE CHIL-
DREN COME TO ME, AND DO NOT HINDER
THEM, FOR THE KINGDOM OF HEAVEN
BELONGS TO SUCH AS THESE."**

MATTHEW 19:14 NIV

Quote #45

TO NOT BE AFRAID.

"FOR THE SPIRIT GOD DOES NOT MAKE US TIMID, BUT GIVES US POWER, LOVE AND SELF-DISCIPLINE."

2 TIMOTHY 1:7 NIV

Quote #46

TO BE BOLD.

"HE PROCLAIMED THE KINGDOM OF GOD AND TAUGHT ABOUT THE LORD JESUS CHRIST— WITH ALL BOLDNESS AND WITHOUT HINDRANCE!"

ACTS 28:31 NIV

Quote #47

TO NOT HATE.

**"WHOEVER CLAIMS TO LOVE GOD
YET HATES A BROTHER OR SISTER IS
A LIAR. WHOEVER DOES NOT LOVE
THEIR BROTHER AND SISTER, WHOM
THEY HAVE SEEN, CANNOT LOVE GOD,
WHOM THEY HAVE NOT SEEN."**

1 JOHN 4:20 NIV

Quote #48

TO NOT GOSSIP.

"A GOSSIP BETRAYS A CONFIDENCE; SO AVOID ANYONE WHO TALKS TOO MUCH."

PROVERBS 20:19 NIV

Quote #49

TO NOT JUDGE.

"FOR IN THE SAME WAY YOU JUDGE OTHERS, YOU WILL BE JUDGED, AND WITH THE MEASURE YOU USE, IT WILL BE MEASURED TO YOU."

MATTHEW 7:2 NIV

Quote #50

TO NOT WORRY.

"DO NOT BE ANXIOUS ABOUT ANYTHING, BUT IN EVERY SITUATION, BY PRAYER AND PETITION, WITH THANKSGIVING, PRESENT YOUR REQUESTS TO GOD."

PHILIPPIANS 4:6 NIV

Quote #51

TO NOT KILL.

"YOU SHALL NOT MURDER."

EXODUS 20:13 NIV

Quote #52

TO NOT LIE.

**"A FALSE WITNESS WILL NOT GO UN-
PUNISHED, AND WHOEVER POURS
OUT LIES WILL NOT GO FREE."**

PROVERBS 19:5 NIV

Quote #53

NOT JUST A PRACTICE, IT'S A RELATION- SHIP WITH GOD.

"HERE I AM! I STAND AT THE DOOR AND KNOCK. IF ANYONE HEARS MY VOICE AND OPENS THE DOOR, I WILL COME IN AND EAT WITH THAT PERSON, AND THEY WITH ME."

REVELATION 3:20 NIV

Quote #54

TO NOT HAVE JEALOUSY IN YOUR HEART.

"FOR WHERE YOU HAVE ENVY AND SELFISH AMBITION, THERE YOU FIND DISORDER AND EVERY EVIL PRACTICE."

JAMES 3:16 NIV

Quote #55

TO NOT CARRY REVENGE TOWARDS ONE ANOTHER.

"DO NOT TAKE REVENGE, MY DEAR FRIENDS, BUT LEAVE ROOM FOR GOD'S WRATH, FOR IT IS WRITTEN: IT IS MINE TO AVENGE; I WILL REPAY," SAYS THE LORD.

ROMANS 12:19 NIV

Quote #56

TO ADVANCE THE KINGDOM OF GOD HERE ON EARTH.

"IN THOSE DAYS JOHN THE BAPTIST CAME, PREACHING IN THE WILDERNESS OF JUDEA."

MATTHEW 3:1 NIV

Quote #57

TO SPREAD THE GOOD NEWS OF JESUS CHRIST.

"FOR I AM NOT ASHAMED OF THE GOSPEL, BECAUSE IT IS THE POWER OF GOD THAT BRINGS SALVATION TO EVERYONE WHO BELIEVES: FIRST TO THE JEW, THEN TO THE GENTILE."

ROMANS 1:16 NIV

Quote #58

TO GLORIFY GOD WITH YOUR GIFTS AND TALENTS.

"EACH OF YOU SHOULD USE WHATEVER GIFT YOU HAVE RECEIVED TO SERVE OTHERS, AS FAITHFUL STEWARDS OF GOD'S GRACE IN ITS VARIOUS FORMS."

1 PETER 4:10 NIV

Quote #59

NOT ABOUT YOU, BUT THE CALLING.

"JUST AS THE SON OF MAN DID NOT COME TO BE SERVED, BUT TO SERVE, AND TO GIVE HIS LIFE AS A RANSOM FOR MANY."

MATTHEW 20:28 NIV

Quote #60

TO TELL OTHERS ABOUT CHRIST.

HE SAID TO THEM, "GO INTO ALL THE WORLD AND PREACH THE GOSPEL TO ALL CREATION."

MARK 16:15 NIV

Quote #61

TO SERVE OTHERS.

**"IN THE SAME WAY, LET YOUR LIGHT
SHINE BEFORE OTHERS, THAT THEY
MAY SEE YOUR GOOD DEEDS AND
GLORIFY YOUR FATHER IN HEAVEN."**

MATTHEW 5:16 NIV

Quote #62

TO NOT WORSHIP IDOLS.

**"DEAR CHILDREN, KEEP YOUR-
SELVES FROM IDOLS."**

1 JOHN 5:21 NIV

Quote #63

TO NOT BE A LOVER OF MONEY.

www.robenschery.com

"KEEP YOUR LIVES FREE FROM THE LOVE OF MONEY AND BE CONTENT WITH WHAT YOU HAVE, BECAUSE GOD HAS SAID, NEVER WILL I LEAVE YOU; NEVER WILL I FORSAKE YOU."

HEBREWS 13:5 NIV

Quote #64

TO NOT INDULGE IN THE LUST OF THE WORLD.

"SO I SAY, WALK BY THE SPIRIT, AND YOU WILL NOT GRATIFY THE DESIRES OF THE FLESH."

GALATIANS 5:16 NIV

Quote #65

TO CONTROL WHAT COMES OUT OF YOUR MOUTH.

"THE TONGUE HAS THE POWER OF LIFE AND DEATH, AND THOSE WHO LOVE IT WILL EAT ITS FRUIT."

PROVERBS 18:21 NIV

Quote #66

TO BE AWARE OF WHAT YOU WATCH.

"I WILL NOT LOOK WITH APPROVAL ON ANYTHING THAT IS VILE. I HATE WHAT FAITHLESS PEOPLE DO; I WILL HAVE NO PART IN IT."

PSALMS 101:3 NIV

Quote #67

TO CONTROL YOUR ANGER.

www.robenschery.com

"HE THAT IS SLOW TO WRATH IS OF GREAT UNDERSTANDING: BUT HE THAT IS HASTY OF SPIRIT EXALTETH FOLLY."

PROVERBS 14:29 KJV

Quote #68

TO BE SET APART FOR SERVICE.

"KNOW THAT THE LORD HAS SET APART HIS FAITHFUL SERVANT FOR HIMSELF; THE LORD HEARS WHEN I CALL TO HIM."

PSALMS 4:3 NIV

Quote #69

TO HEAL THE SICK.

**"HEAL THE SICK, RAISE THE DEAD,
CLEANSE THOSE WHO HAVE LEPROSY,
DRIVE OUT DEMONS. FREELY YOU
HAVE RECEIVED; FREELY GIVE."**

MATTHEW 10:8 NIV

Quote #70

TO SET THE CAPTIVE FREE.

"THE SPIRIT OF THE LORD IS ON ME, BECAUSE HE HAS ANOINTED ME TO PRO-CLAIM GOOD NEWS TO THE POOR. HE HAS SENT ME TO PROCLAIM FREEDOM FOR THE PRISONERS AND RECOVERY OF SIGHT FOR THE BLIND, TO SET THE OPPRESSED FREE."

LUKE 4:18 NIV

Quote #71

TO TAKE CARE OF YOUR PHYSICAL BODY.

"DO YOU NOT KNOW THAT YOUR BODIES ARE TEMPLES OF THE HOLY SPIRIT, WHO IS IN YOU, WHOM YOU HAVE RECEIVED FROM GOD? YOU ARE NOT YOUR OWN."

1 CORINTHIANS 6:19 NIV

Quote #72

TO LOVE YOUR WIFE/ HUSBAND UNCON- DITIONALLY.

"HOWEVER, EACH ONE OF YOU ALSO MUST LOVE HIS WIFE AS HE LOVES HIMSELF, AND THE WIFE MUST RESPECT HER HUSBAND."

EPHESIANS 5:33 NIV

Quote #73

TO LOVE THE UNLOVABLE.

"BUT I TELL YOU, LOVE YOUR ENEMIES AND PRAY FOR THOSE WHO PERSECUTE YOU."

MATTHEW 5:44 NIV

Quote #74

TO CARE FOR YOUR CHILDREN.

"ANYONE WHO DOES NOT PROVIDE FOR THEIR RELATIVES, AND ESPE-CIALLY FOR THEIR OWN HOUSE-HOLD, HAS DENIED THE FAITH AND IS WORSE THAN AN UNBELIEVER."

1 TIMOTHY 5:8 NIV

Quote #75

TO CARE FOR
THE ELDERLY.

**"LET THE ELDERS WHO RULE
WELL BE CONSIDERED WORTHY OF DOUBLE
HONOR, ESPECIALLY THOSE WHO LABOR
IN PREACHING AND TEACHING."**

1 TIMOTHY 5:17

Quote #76

TO CARE FOR THE WIDOWS.

"IF ANY WOMAN WHO IS A BELIEVER HAS WIDOWS IN HER CARE, SHE SHOULD CONTINUE TO HELP THEM AND NOT LET THE CHURCH BE BURDENED WITH THEM, SO THAT THE CHURCH CAN HELP THOSE WIDOWS WHO ARE REALLY IN NEED."

1 TIMOTHY 5:16 NIV

Quote #77

TO HONOR YOUR PARENTS.

"CHILDREN, OBEY YOUR PARENTS IN THE LORD, FOR THIS IS RIGHT. HONOR YOUR FATHER AND MOTHER WHICH IS THE FIRST COMMANDMENT WITH A PROMISE."

EPHESIANS 6:1-2 NIV

Quote #78

TO DISPLAY KINDNESS.

www.robenschery.com

"BE KIND AND COMPASSIONATE TO ONE ANOTHER, FORGIVING EACH OTHER, JUST AS IN CHRIST GOD FORGAVE YOU."

EPHESIANS 4:32 NIV

Quote #79

TO LOVE BEYOND BORDERS.

"LOVE DOES NOT DELIGHT IN EVIL BUT REJOICES WITH THE TRUTH. IT ALWAYS PROTECTS, ALWAYS TRUSTS, ALWAYS HOPES, ALWAYS PERSEVERES."

1 CORINTHIANS 13:6-7 NIV

Quote #80

TO NOT HATE THOSE WHO SPEAK AGAINST YOU.

"BUT TO YOU WHO ARE LISTENING I SAY: LOVE YOUR ENEMIES, DO GOOD TO THOSE WHO HATE YOU, BLESS THOSE WHO CURSE YOU, PRAY FOR THOSE WHO MISTREAT YOU."

LUKE 6:27-28

Quote #81

TO BLESS OTHERS NOT CURSE THEM.

"BLESS THOSE WHO PERSECUTE YOU; BLESS AND DO NOT CURSE."

ROMANS 12:14 NIV

Quote #82

TO LIVE IN PEACE WITH EVERYONE.

"IF IT IS POSSIBLE, AS FAR AS IT DEPENDS ON YOU, LIVE AT PEACE WITH EVERYONE."

ROMANS 12:18 NIV

Quote #83

TO NOT TAKE GOD'S GRACE FOR GRANTED.

"WHAT SHALL WE SAY, THEN? SHALL WE GO ON SINNING SO THAT GRACE MAY INCREASE?"

ROMANS 6:1 NIV

Quote #84

TO BE THANKFUL.

**"GIVE THANKS IN ALL CIRCUM-
STANCES; FOR THIS IS GOD'S WILL
FOR YOU IN CHRIST JESUS."**

1 THESSALONIANS 5:18 NIV

Quote #85

TO GLORIFY GOD WITH YOUR WEALTH.

"HONOR THE LORD WITH YOUR WEALTH, WITH THE FIRST FRUITS OF ALL YOUR CROPS."

PROVERBS 3:9 NIV

Quote #86

TO GIVE WITH NO STRINGS ATTACHED.

"EACH OF YOU SHOULD GIVE WHAT YOU HAVE DECIDED IN YOUR HEART TO GIVE, NOT RELUCTANTLY OR UNDER COMPULSION, FOR GOD LOVES A CHEERFUL GIVER."

2 CORINTHIANS 9:7 NIV

Quote #87

TO LIVE A SACRIFICIAL LIFE DAILY.

THEN PETER SPOKE UP, "WE HAVE LEFT EVERYTHING TO FOLLOW YOU!"

MARK 10:28 NIV

Quote #88

TO SPREAD THE GOSPEL NOT YOUR OPINIONS.

"THEREFORE GO AND MAKE DISCIPLES OF ALL NATIONS, BAPTIZING THEM IN THE NAME OF THE FATHER AND OF THE SON AND OF THE HOLY SPIRIT."

MATTHEW 28:19 NIV

Quote #89

TO NOT BE ASHAMED OF THE GOSPEL OF JESUS CHRIST.

"FOR I AM NOT ASHAMED OF THE GOSPEL, BECAUSE IT IS THE POWER OF GOD THAT BRINGS SALVATION TO EVERYONE WHO BELIEVES: FIRST TO THE JEW, THEN TO THE GENTILE."

ROMANS 1:16 NIV

Quote #90

TO NOT PRACTICE FORNICATION.

"FLEE FROM SEXUAL IMMORAL- ITY. ALL OTHER SINS A PERSON COMMITS ARE OUTSIDE THE BODY, BUT WHOEVER SINS SEXUALLY, SINS AGAINST THEIR OWN BODY."

1 CORINTHIANS 6:18 NIV

Quote #91

TO NOT PRACTICE ADULTERY.

"MARRIAGE SHOULD BE HONORED BY ALL, AND THE MARRIAGE BED KEPT PURE, FOR GOD WILL JUDGE THE ADULTERER AND ALL THE SEXUALLY IMMORAL."

HEBREWS 13:4 NIV

Quote #92

TO HAVE A SOBER MIND.

**"BE ALERT AND OF SOBER MIND. YOUR
ENEMY THE DEVIL PROWLS AROUND
LIKE A ROARING LION LOOKING
FOR SOMEONE TO DEVOUR."**

1 PETER 5:8 NIV

Quote #93

TO BE GRATEFUL FOR GOD'S GOODNESS.

www.robenschery.com

**"PRAISE THE LORD. GIVE THANKS
TO THE LORD, FOR HE IS GOOD;
HIS LOVE ENDURES FOREVER."**

PSALMS 106:1 NIV

Quote #94

TO RESPECT OTHERS AS YOURSELF.

**"SO IN EVERYTHING, DO TO OTHERS
WHAT YOU WOULD HAVE THEM DO
TO YOU, FOR THIS SUMS UP THE
LAW AND THE PROPHETS."**

MATTHEW 7:12 NIV

Quote #95

TO BE COMPASSIONATE TOWARDS OTHERS.

**"CARRY EACH OTHER'S BURDENS,
AND IN THIS WAY YOU WILL
FULFILL THE LAW OF CHRIST."**

GALATIANS 6:2 NIV

Quote #96

TO BELIEVE IN THE TRINITY.

"YET FOR US THERE IS BUT ONE GOD, THE FATHER, FROM WHOM ALL THINGS CAME AND FOR WHOM WE LIVE; AND THERE IS BUT ONE LORD, JESUS CHRIST, THROUGH WHOM ALL THINGS CAME AND THROUGH WHOM WE LIVE."

1 CORINTHIANS 8:6

Quote #97

TO CARE FOR THE ORPHANS.

"RELIGION THAT GOD OUR FATHER ACCEPTS AS PURE AND FAULTLESS IS THIS: TO LOOK AFTER ORPHANS AND WIDOWS IN THEIR DISTRESS AND TO KEEP ONESELF FROM BEING POLLUTED BY THE WORLD."

JAMES 1:27 NIV

Quote #98

TO BE LIKE CHRIST.

"THEREFORE BE IMITATORS OF GOD, AS BELOVED CHILDREN."

EPHESIANS 5:1 ESV

Quote #99

TO LIVE FOR CHRIST.

"I HAVE BEEN CRUCIFIED WITH CHRIST. IT IS NO LONGER I WHO LIVE, BUT CHRIST WHO LIVES IN ME. AND THE LIFE I NOW LIVE IN THE FLESH I LIVE BY FAITH IN THE SON OF GOD, WHO LOVED ME AND GAVE HIMSELF FOR ME."

GALATIANS 2:20 ESV

Quote #100

NOT TO BE LUKEWARM.

"I KNOW YOUR WORKS: YOU ARE NEITHER COLD NOR HOT. WOULD THAT YOU WERE EITHER COLD OR HOT! SO, BECAUSE YOU ARE LUKEWARM, AND NEITHER HOT NOR COLD, I WILL SPIT YOU OUT OF MY MOUTH."

REVELATION 3:15-16 ESV

Quote #101

TO STAND AGAINST CRUELTY.

"WHOEVER SHUTS THEIR EARS TO THE CRY OF THE POOR WILL ALSO CRY OUT AND NOT BE ANSWERED."

PROVERBS 21:13 NIV

Quote #102

TO SPEAK AGAINST INJUSTICE.

www.robenschery.com

"ACQUITTING THE GUILTY AND CONDEMNING THE INNOCENT THE LORD DETESTS THEM BOTH."

PROVERBS 17:15 NIV

Quote #103

TO NOT ALLOW YOUR CULTURE TO BE YOUR GOD.

"DO NOT CONFORM TO THE PATTERN OF THIS WORLD, BUT BE TRANSFORMED BY THE RENEWING OF YOUR MIND. THEN YOU WILL BE ABLE TO TEST AND APPROVE WHAT GOD'S WILL IS—HIS GOOD, PLEASING AND PERFECT WILL."

ROMANS 12:2 NIV

Quote #104

TO NOT LIVE IN FEAR.

**"FOR THE SPIRIT OF GOD DOES NOT
MAKE US TIMID, BUT GIVES US POWER,
LOVE AND SELF-DISCIPLINE."**

2 TIMOTHY 1:7 NIV

Quote #105

TO COMMIT YOUR WAYS TO GOD.

www.robenschery.com

**"COMMIT YOUR WAY TO THE LORD;
TRUST IN HIM AND HE WILL DO THIS."**

PSALMS 37:5 NIV

Quote #106

TO HAVE A RELATION-SHIP WITH GOD.

"HERE I AM! I STAND AT THE DOOR AND KNOCK. IF ANYONE HEARS MY VOICE AND OPENS THE DOOR, I WILL COME IN AND EAT WITH THAT PERSON, AND THEY WITH ME."

REVELATION 3:20 NIV

Quote #107

TO BE WILLING TO CHANGE FROM YOUR WAYS TO GOD'S WAYS.

www.robenschery.com

"LET THE WICKED FORSAKE THEIR WAYS AND THE UNRIGHTEOUS THEIR THOUGHTS. LET THEM TURN TO THE LORD, AND HE WILL HAVE MERCY ON THEM, AND TO OUR GOD, FOR HE WILL FREELY PARDON."

ISAIAH 55:7 NIV

Quote #108

TO TELL THE TRUTH IN LOVE.

"THEREFORE EACH OF YOU MUST PUT OFF FALSEHOOD AND SPEAK TRUTH- FULLY TO YOUR NEIGHBOR, FOR WE ARE ALL MEMBERS OF ONE BODY."

EPHESIANS 4:25 NIV

Quote #109

TO NOT BE CONFUSED ABOUT YOUR IDENTITY.

"I PRAISE YOU BECAUSE I AM FEAR-FULLY AND WONDERFULLY MADE; YOUR WORKS ARE WONDERFUL, I KNOW THAT FULL WELL."

PSALMS 139:14 NIV

Quote #110

TO BE READY AT ALL TIMES FOR THE SECOND COMING OF JESUS CHRIST.

"FOR YOU KNOW VERY WELL THAT THE DAY OF THE LORD WILL COME LIKE A THIEF IN THE NIGHT."

1 THESSALONIANS 5:2 NIV

Quote #111

TO HONOR GOD WITH YOUR BODY.

"DO YOU NOT KNOW THAT YOUR BODIES ARE TEMPLES OF THE HOLY SPIRIT, WHO IS IN YOU, WHOM YOU HAVE RECEIVED FROM GOD? YOU ARE NOT YOUR OWN."

1 CORINTHIANS 6:19 NIV

Quote #112

TO USE YOUR MOUTH TO SPEAK LIFE INSTEAD OF DEATH.

"THE TONGUE HAS THE POWER OF LIFE AND DEATH, AND THOSE WHO LOVE IT WILL EAT ITS FRUIT."

PROVERBS 18:21 NIV

Quote #113

TO WATCH OVER THE WORDS THAT COME OUT OF YOUR MOUTH.

"THOSE WHO GUARD THEIR LIPS PRE-SERVE THEIR LIVES, BUT THOSE WHO SPEAK RASHLY WILL COME TO RUIN."

PROVERBS 13:3 NIV

Quote #114

TO HAVE FAITH IN CHRIST NOT MEN.

"I HAVE BEEN CRUCIFIED WITH CHRIST AND I NO LONGER LIVE, BUT CHRIST LIVES IN ME. THE LIFE I NOW LIVE IN THE BODY, I LIVE BY FAITH IN THE SON OF GOD, WHO LOVED ME AND GAVE HIMSELF FOR ME."

GALATIANS 2:20 NIV

Quote #115

TO NOT WORRY ABOUT LIFE'S STRUGGLES.

www.robenschery.com

"DO NOT BE ANXIOUS ABOUT ANYTHING, BUT IN EVERY SITUATION, BY PRAYER AND PETITION, WITH THANKSGIVING, PRESENT YOUR REQUESTS TO GOD."

PHILIPPIANS 4:6 NIV

Quote #116

TO HATE WHAT JESUS HATES.

"LOVE MUST BE SINCERE. HATE WHAT IS EVIL; CLING TO WHAT IS GOOD."

ROMANS 12:9 NIV

Quote #117

TO REMAIN WHO WE ARE AND LOVE THOSE WHO DON'T LIKE WHO WE ARE.

www.robenschery.com

"A NEW COMMAND I GIVE YOU: LOVE ONE ANOTHER AS I HAVE LOVED YOU, SO YOU MUST LOVE ONE ANOTHER. BY THIS, EVERYONE WILL KNOW THAT YOU ARE MY DISCIPLES, IF YOU LOVE ONE ANOTHER."

JOHN 13:34-35 NIV

Quote #118

TO LOVE WHAT JESUS LOVES.

"AND SO WE KNOW AND RELY ON THE LOVE GOD HAS FOR US. GOD IS LOVE. WHOEVER LIVES IN LOVE LIVES IN GOD, AND GOD IN THEM."

1 JOHN 4:16 NIV

Quote #119

TO BE TRANSFORMED.

**"AND WE ALL, WHO WITH UNVEILED
FACES CONTEMPLATE THE LORD'S
GLORY, ARE BEING TRANSFORMED
INTO HIS IMAGE WITH EVER-INCREAS-
ING GLORY, WHICH COMES FROM
THE LORD, WHO IS THE SPIRIT."**

2 CORINTHIANS 3:18 NIV

Quote #120

TO BELIEVE THAT JESUS CHRIST IS THE GOOD NEWS.

"THE BEGINNING OF THE GOOD NEWS ABOUT JESUS THE MESSIAH, THE SON OF GOD."

MARK 1:1 NIV

Quote #121

TO BELIEVE THAT JESUS LOVES EVERYONE, BUT HATES THEIR SINS.

www.robenschery.com

"BUT GOD DEMONSTRATES HIS OWN LOVE FOR US IN THIS: WHILE WE WERE STILL SINNERS, CHRIST DIED FOR US."

ROMANS 5:8 NIV

Quote #122

TO BELIEVE IN THE RESURRECTION OF JESUS CHRIST.

JESUS SAID TO HER, "I AM THE RES-URRECTION AND THE LIFE. THE ONE WHO BELIEVES IN ME WILL LIVE, EVEN THOUGH THEY DIE."

JOHN 11:25 NIV

Quote #123

TO BEHAVE IN A GODLY MANNER.

"FINALLY, BROTHERS AND SISTERS, WHATEVER IS TRUE, WHATEVER IS NOBLE, WHATEVER IS RIGHT, WHATEVER IS PURE, WHATEVER IS LOVELY, WHATEVER IS ADMIRABLE—IF ANYTHING IS EXCELLENT OR PRAISEWORTHY THINK ABOUT SUCH THINGS."

PHILIPPIANS 4:8 NIV

Quote #124

IS SOMEONE WHOSE HEART REFLECTS JESUS CHRIST.

"AS WATER REFLECTS THE FACE, SO ONE'S LIFE REFLECTS THE HEART."

PROVERBS 27:19 NIV

Quote #125

TO HONOR GOD WITH YOUR RESOURCES.

"HONOR THE LORD WITH YOUR WEALTH, WITH THE FIRST FRUITS OF ALL YOUR CROPS."

PROVERBS 3:9 NIV

Quote #126

TO GROW.

**"WHEN I WAS A CHILD, I TALKED LIKE
A CHILD, I THOUGHT LIKE A CHILD,
I REASONED LIKE A CHILD. WHEN
I BECAME A MAN, I PUT THE WAYS
OF CHILDHOOD BEHIND ME."**

1 CORINTHIANS 13:11 NIV

Quote #127

TO CARE FOR THE POOR.

"WHOEVER IS KIND TO THE POOR LENDS TO THE LORD, AND HE WILL REWARD THEM FOR WHAT THEY HAVE DONE."

PROVERBS 19:17 NIV

Quote #128

TO CAST YOUR CARES AND BURDENS ON GOD.

**"CAST ALL YOUR ANXIETY ON HIM
BECAUSE HE CARES FOR YOU."**

1 PETER 5:7 NIV

Quote #129

TO UNDERSTAND THE PRINCIPLE OF GIVING.

www.robenschery.com

"EACH OF YOU SHOULD GIVE WHAT YOU HAVE DECIDED IN YOUR HEART TO GIVE, NOT RELUCTANTLY OR UNDER COMPUL- SION, FOR GOD LOVES A CHEERFUL GIVER."

2 CORINTHIANS 9:7 NIV

Quote #130

TO HAVE THE MINDSET OF JESUS.

"THEN MAKE MY JOY COMPLETE BY BEING LIKE-MINDED, HAVING THE SAME LOVE, BEING ONE IN SPIRIT AND OF ONE MIND."

PHILIPPIANS 2:2 NIV

Quote #131

NOT TO STEAL.

www.robenschery.com

**"ANYONE WHO HAS BEEN STEALING MUST
STEAL NO LONGER, BUT MUST WORK,
DOING SOMETHING USEFUL WITH THEIR
OWN HANDS, THAT THEY MAY HAVE SOME-
THING TO SHARE WITH THOSE IN NEED."**

EPHESIANS 4:28 NIV

Quote #132

TO LIVE A LIFE
OF HONOR.

**"PRAY FOR US. WE ARE SURE THAT WE
HAVE A CLEAR CONSCIENCE AND DESIRE
TO LIVE HONORABLY IN EVERY WAY."**

HEBREWS 13:18 NIV

Quote #133

TO KNOW THAT GOD WILL NEVER FORSAKE YOU.

"THE LORD HIMSELF GOES BEFORE YOU AND WILL BE WITH YOU; HE WILL NEVER LEAVE YOU NOR FORSAKE YOU. DO NOT BE AFRAID; DO NOT BE DISCOURAGED."

DEUTERONOMY 31:8 NIV

Quote #134

TO NOT HOLD GRUDGES.

**"GET RID OF ALL BITTERNESS, RAGE
AND ANGER, BRAWLING AND SLANDER,
ALONG WITH EVERY FORM OF MALICE."**

EPHESIANS 4:31 NIV

Quote #135

TO NOT TAKE VENGEANCE AGAINST YOUR NEIGHBORS.

"DO NOT SEEK REVENGE OR BEAR A GRUDGE AGAINST ANYONE AMONG YOUR PEOPLE, BUT LOVE YOUR NEIGHBOR AS YOURSELF. I AM THE LORD."

LEVITICUS 19:18 NIV

Quote #136

TO NOT WORRY.

**"DO NOT BE ANXIOUS ABOUT ANYTHING,
BUT IN EVERY SITUATION, BY PRAYER
AND PETITION, WITH THANKSGIVING,
PRESENT YOUR REQUESTS TO GOD."**

PHILIPPIANS 4:6 NIV

Quote #137

TO KNOW THAT YOU ARE AN OVERCOMER.

www.robenschery.com

"I HAVE TOLD YOU THESE THINGS, SO THAT IN ME YOU MAY HAVE PEACE. IN THIS WORLD YOU WILL HAVE TROUBLE. BUT TAKE HEART! I HAVE OVERCOME THE WORLD."

JOHN 16:33 NIV

Quote #138

TO BE REDEEMED.

"WHO GAVE HIMSELF FOR US TO REDEEM US FROM ALL WICKEDNESS AND TO PURIFY FOR HIMSELF A PEOPLE THAT ARE HIS VERY OWN, EAGER TO DO WHAT IS GOOD."

TITUS 2:14 NIV

Quote #139

TO BE RESTORED.

**"AND THE GOD OF ALL GRACE, WHO
CALLED YOU TO HIS ETERNAL GLORY
IN CHRIST, AFTER YOU HAVE SUF-
FERED A LITTLE WHILE, WILL HIMSELF
RESTORE YOU AND MAKE YOU
STRONG, FIRM AND STEADFAST."**

1 PETER 5:10 NIV

Quote #140

TO BE RECONCILED TO CHRIST.

"ALL THIS IS FROM GOD, WHO REC-ONCILED US TO HIMSELF THROUGH CHRIST AND GAVE US THE MINIS-TRY OF RECONCILIATION."

2 CORINTHIANS 5:18 NIV

Quote #141

TO KNOW THAT ALL THINGS ARE POSSIBLE THROUGH CHRIST.

www.robenschery.com

JESUS LOOKED AT THEM AND SAID, "WITH MAN THIS IS IMPOSSIBLE, BUT WITH GOD ALL THINGS ARE POSSIBLE."

MATTHEW 19:26 NIV

Quote #142

TO DO MISSION WORK.

**"EACH OF YOU SHOULD USE WHATEV-
ER GIFT YOU HAVE RECEIVED TO SERVE
OTHERS, AS FAITHFUL STEWARDS OF
GOD'S GRACE IN ITS VARIOUS FORMS."**

1 PETER 4:10

Quote #143

TO LIVE A LIFESTYLE OF EVANGELISM.

"DO YOUR BEST TO PRESENT YOUR-SELF TO GOD AS ONE APPROVED, A WORKER WHO DOES NOT NEED TO BE ASHAMED AND WHO CORRECTLY HANDLES THE WORD OF TRUTH."

2 TIMOTHY 2:15

Quote #144

TO DO UNTO OTHERS AS YOU WOULD WANT TO BE DONE TO YOU.

"DO TO OTHERS AS YOU WOULD HAVE THEM DO TO YOU."

LUKE 6:31 NIV

CONCLUSION

With love, you can be a triumphant Christian and be Christ-like.

"If I speak in the tongues of men or of angels, but do not have love, I am only a resounding gong or a clanging cymbal. If I have the gift of prophecy and can fathom all mysteries and all knowledge, and if I have a faith that can move mountains, but do not have love, I am nothing. If I give all I possess to the poor and give over my body to hardship that I may boast, but do not have love, I gain nothing. Love is patient, love is kind. It does not envy, it does not boast, it is not proud. It does not dishonor others, it is not self-seeking, it is not easily angered, it keeps no record of wrongs. Love does not delight in evil but rejoices with the truth. It always protects, always trusts, always hopes, always perseveres." *1 Corinthians 13:1-7 NIV*

Looking at all these quotes, a person may say to be a Christian is just too much to do. To be a Christian is just too much because there are so many rules to follow. I want to say to that person, to be a Christian is a lifestyle. To be a Christian is a way of thinking. Once you change your mindset, being a Christian can be easier than you can imagine. As Christians, the goal is to grow daily and not remain in the same spiritual state you were in when you gave your life to Christ.

The goal for this book is to serve as a daily reminder of our Christian faith. Allow the words, quotes, and scriptures to penetrate your mind and heart. Jesus said, "If you love me, you will follow my commands." Let us follow Christ with all of our hearts. The Christian walk is not perfect; however we are called to be perfected by Christ Jesus. After reading the quotes and scriptures in this book, I have a few questions for you.

Do you want to be a Christian? Why or why not?

_____

_____

_____

_____

_____

Do you want to accept Jesus Christ as your Lord and savior? If so, how do you plan on connecting with a local bible believing congregation?

_____

_____

_____

_____

_____

Do you want to recommit your life to Christ?

_____

_____

_____

_____

Do you want to be baptized?

_____

_____

_____

If you need a community to grow in Christ or more guidance about the faith, please connect with me at
Hello@robenschery.com
    Robenschery.com
    Rc ministries on Facebook
    robenschery on Instagram

Definition of Christian on pg. xiv

Merriam-Webster. (n.d.). Citation. In Merriam-Webster.com dictionary. Retrieved January 20, 2023, from https://www.merriam-webster.com/dictionary/citation

Made in the USA
Columbia, SC
17 October 2023